Impressions of
HACKNEY
1861–2001

The Swan public house, *c.* 1886. (*Alfred Braddock – AB*)

The Swan public house, Clapton Common, 2001. (*David Mander – DM*)

Impressions of HACKNEY
1861–2001

DAVID MANDER, MICHAEL KIRKLAND & MARTIN TAYLOR

S U T T O N   P U B L I S H I N G

Sutton Publishing Limited
Phoenix Mill · Thrupp · Stroud
Gloucestershire · GL5 2BU

First published 2002

Half-title page: Photomontage of Congress Hall, Lower
Clapton, *c.* 1905. (*HAD*) and the Portico, Lower Clapton,
2001. (*MK*). *Title and contents pages*: The Plough public
house, Homerton, *c.* 1870 (*GJ*) and 2001 (*MK*). *Endpapers*:
Deprived children at the Hoxton Market Christian Mission,
1900 (*HAD*).

British Library Cataloguing in Publication Data
A catalogue record for this book is available from the British
Library.

ISBN 0-7509-2769-0

Typeset in 10.5/13.5 Photina.
Typesetting and origination by
Sutton Publishing Limited.
Printed and bound in England by
J.H. Haynes & Co. Ltd, Sparkford.

This book is dedicated to Jenny, Yvonne, Daniel, Amelia and Lilian.

Key to photographers

(*GJ*)	George James
(*AB*)	Alfred Braddock
(*CM*)	Charles Martin
(*LMA*)	London Metropolitan Archives
(*HAD*)	Hackney Archives Department
(*DM*)	David Mander
(*MK*)	Michael Kirkland

*All the photographs are subject to copyright. Thanks must go to the London Metropolitan Archives for
permission to use the old photograph in the montage on page 91.*

Hoxton Hall, Shoreditch, *c.* 1906. (*HAD*)

Hoxton Hall, Shoreditch, 2001. (*DM*)

Contents

Lea Bridge, Lower Clapton, *c.* 1870. (*HAD*)

Princess of Wales public house, Lea Bridge, 2001. (*MK*)

INTRODUCTION

Welcome to *Impressions of Hackney: 1861–2001*. This fifth selection of historic photographs, taken mainly from the collection at Hackney Archives Department, has been produced as a 'then and now' photographic survey of Hackney by popular demand. A previous collection, *A Second Look*, published by Centerprise in 1975, was the work of the late Israel Renson and Michael Silvey. That book took a selection of the photographs of Alfred Braddock covering parts of the old metropolitan borough of Hackney, and while *Impressions of Hackney 1861–2001* pays homage to its illustrious predecessor, we have added pictures from the camera of George James and a range of other photographers working before the First World War, to extend the historic photographs back in time to the Hackney of the 1860s, and to include a representative range of views for Shoreditch and Stoke Newington.

The book is a collaborative effort by the staff of Hackney Archives Department compiled in their own time. Original picture research was a combined effort. The new photographs, all shot on digital cameras in the spring and summer of 2001, were taken by Michael Kirkland and David Mander. Martin Taylor undertook the research for the captions except for Lower Clapton, Homerton and the River Lea, which was done by Michael Kirkland. The photo-montages – blending historic and contemporary views for the cover and for some of the views in the book – were the work of Michael Kirkland. The book also represents the swan song of the present team, two of whom left Hackney Archives Department for new career opportunities at the end of September 2001.

As with the first chapter of *Hackney, Homerton and Dalston in Old Photographs*, this book has been arranged in the form of a very long walk round the borough. Starting in Stoke Newington, the reader is taken on a journey through Stamford Hill, Upper Clapton, along the Lea, then via Lower Clapton and Homerton to Mare Street. From Pembury Road we go on to Hackney Downs and then via Shacklewell to Dalston, De Beauvoir Town and Shoreditch. The tour's end, via Broadway Market, is South Hackney, a former stamping ground of two of the authors.

The new photographs have captured some of the atmosphere of the multi-cultural Hackney of today; the book is a record of change and growth. In some instances only the shape of the road remains of the Victorian view, in others we were surprised to find stalwart survivors from the nineteenth century. All the old photographs have been scanned and can be seen on the Archives Department's Hackney on Disk database, and the photographs of 2001 will be added in due course.

It only remains to wish the reader a happy voyage, and to thank Martin Taylor and Michael Kirkland for all their hard work at Hackney Archives Department over the last four and five years respectively.

David Mander
September 2001

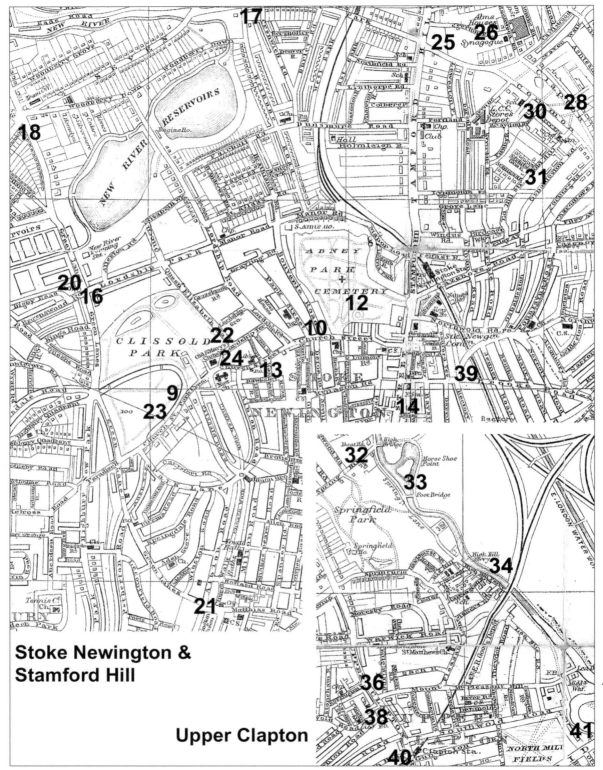

Map 1: Stoke Newington, Stamford Hill and Upper Clapton, *c.* 1935. Numbers show the location of photographs and refer to page numbers.

Stoke Newington, Stamford Hill & Upper Clapton

Montage of the Grange and New River *c.* 1920 (*HAD*) and Stoke Newington
Church Street. (*MK*)

Far less congested than it is today was Stoke Newington Church Street, seen here in about 1890. It still retains its character as a semi-rural village street, a character the modern estate agents of these parts would have us believe it still retains. In the middle distance stands the Red Lion, an inn that was on this site as early as 1697, although this is probably a later building. On the right the St Mary's Day Nursery offered a meeting place for the mothers of Stoke Newington, and the Amethyst Club next door provided the same function for Stoke Newington's working men from 1882 to 1917. (*HAD*)

Only the building on the left of the picture, at the corner of Marton Road, and that on the corner of Lordship Road, beyond the rebuilt Red Lion, remain from the earlier view. The Red Lion was rebuilt in its present form in 1931, and despite the magnificent beasts remaining on either side of the main door, it has been renamed the Tup in the last few years. Stoke Newington Church Street is the site of the Stoke Newington Festival each summer, a vibrant mix of the music and cuisine of the many different cultures which make up the modern London Borough of Hackney. (*DM*)

Abney Park Cemetery was opened in 1840 in the vanguard of the Victorian 'garden-cemetery' movement. As such, it was always intended that it should be a place of relaxation and contemplation for the living, as well as providing accommodation for the dead. The statue, erected in 1845 and sculpted by E.H. Bailey, is of the hymn writer Isaac Watts. Watts spent the last years of his life (1735–48) at Abney House, on the site of the cemetery, as a guest of its owner, Mary, Lady Abney. (*GJ*)

What the proprietors of the cemetery had not realised was that the Abney Park Cemetery had a life only as long as the number of burials that could be squeezed into the cemetery. After the Second World War the cemetery became increasingly congested, and the chapel, as can be seen, was allowed to decay. The cemetery was sold by the company to Hackney Council in 1978 for £1. The Abney Park Cemetery Trust now runs the cemetery and has revived it as a nature reserve and public open space. (*DM*)

Stoke Newington Church Street, looking east towards the Red Lion in about 1880. In the centre of the picture are the vestry offices at no. 126. Until 1965 Stoke Newington had its own local government; the parish vestry until 1900 and Stoke Newington Metropolitan Borough Council 1900–65. Perhaps for this, as well as any number of other reasons, Stoke Newington has always seemed a rather semi-detached part of the London Borough of Hackney. (*HAD*)

The tall Georgian house on the left of the earlier view survives as Bridgewood and Neitzert's violin shop at no. 116. Little else survives from 1880, as Stoke Newington was built up and rebuilt to meet the demands of an increasing, urban population in the quarter century before the First World War. The sign to Scholars Yard, new apartments and homes, indicates that this process of urban renewal is ongoing. (*DM*)

Stoke Newington High Street is one stretch of the old Roman road from London to York, formerly Ermine Street and now the A10. As this view looking north from about 1900 shows, it was as important a thoroughfare a hundred years ago as it is now – albeit less congested. Until 1965 it was the boundary between Stoke Newington parish and the later borough to the west and Hackney to the east. (*HAD*)

Relatively little has changed to the buildings along this stretch of Stoke Newington High Street in the last century, above the level of the shopfronts. The outstanding landmark on the west side remains the ornate pile of the Rochester Castle pub, newly rebuilt in its present form shortly before the earlier view was taken. There was a pub of this name on this site by 1809. In the mid-nineteenth century it was the meeting place of worthy self help societies such as the True Brothers of Stoke Newington and Hackney Improved Birmingham Benefit Society. Now under the management of Wetherspoons, it is one of Hackney's busy and popular Victorian pubs. Recently a number of pubs across the borough, after many years of struggle, have closed and either been converted to flats or demolished for new housing. (*DM*)

Lordship Park was developed in the late 1860s. The houses seen here being built at the Green Lane end of the road offered 'every convenience for a family', including the option to rent a stable and coach house. (*HAD*)

Many of the imposing Victorian villas of Hackney are now in multi-occupancy. These in Lordship Park offered twelve rooms to be carved up into flats and bedsits. The stone lion on the left hand pillar still guards the entrance to the road. (*DM*)

Amhurst Park was begun in 1864 and extended through to Seven Sisters Road in 1873. The major builder was Jesse Chesham, who lived in the road in 1881. Like most nineteenth-century developments in Stoke Newington it was built to provide homes for the wealthier middle classes. A place of worship for them was provided by the Wesleyan Methodist chapel of 1888. (*HAD*)

The Methodist chapel still dominates the modern view, but since 1956 it has housed the North London Progressive Synagogue. Hackney's Jewish community, particularly the Hassidim of Stamford Hill, is one of the largest ethnic communities in the modern borough. Members of the community have campaigned against Amhurst Park's seamier side – its reputation as a red light district. (*DM*)

17

Above: The Manor House tavern at the junction of Green Lanes and Seven Sisters Road in about 1860. It appears as a handsome Regency building, and the inscription on the south side commemorates a brief stop by Queen Victoria in 1843. From 1852 to 1903 it had a licensed concert room. The gates in the foreground are tollgates; Green Lanes was a turnpike road from 1789. (*HAD*)

Opposite: The Manor House junction was transformed by the construction of the Piccadilly Line underground station, opened in 1932. This entailed the demolition of much of the surrounding area, including the old pub, replaced by the present 1931 building designed by A.W. Blomfield. Also contributing to the change in the area was the construction of Woodberry Down, just east of Manor House, the huge London County Council estate built between 1946 and 1952 to provide decent housing for inner-city dwellers. Critics of the scheme regarded it as an attempt at social engineering by the London County Council; in a phrase attributed to Herbert Morrison, 'to build the Tories out of London'. (*DM*)

The New River ran through Stoke Newington for 200 years before the increasing demands of London led to improvements in water supply in the Victorian period. As part of this process the New River Co. built two reservoirs in Stoke Newington in 1833, and in 1852 laid out filter beds. They also built this (to some modern eyes, magnificently silly), pumping station on Green Lanes to the designs of Robert Billings, in the style that became known as 'Water Board Gothic'. (*HAD*)

The pumping station was redundant from 1936, and the construction of the London ring-main in the 1990s spelled the end for the filter beds and reservoirs. The filter beds were built on, but yet another Stoke Newington campaign secured the West Reservoir for public use. The castellated pumping station, now actually named the Castle, was converted into an indoor climbing centre in 1995. (*DM*)

Newington Green, seen here in about 1889, was one of the oldest parts of Stoke Newington. It was built up from the seventeenth century, and on the west side is London's oldest surviving brick terrace dated 1658. On the north side, seen here, is the Newington Green Unitarian chapel, Hackney's oldest surviving non-Anglican place of worship. It was built in 1708 for a congregation established in 1682, a fitting monument to Hackney's long and continuing tradition of political and religious nonconformity. (HAD)

Some of Newington Green's seventeenth- and eighteenth-century character was lost when Albion Road was widened in 1892. The large Georgian house occupied by the East Highbury Liberal Club in the earlier view was replaced by the London & Provincial Bank. The bank, subsequently a branch of Barclays, now lies derelict. However, with the construction of a block of flats by the Peabody Trust on the opposite corner of the Albion Road junction, Newington Green might experience something of a revival. (DM)

Queen Elizabeth's Walk is seen here on a quiet afternoon in about 1905. Although not built up until the later nineteenth century, it was a public walk much earlier, associated with the eighteenth-century houses in Church Row, on the site of the present Stoke Newington Municipal Offices. It takes its name from the first Queen Elizabeth, who is supposed to have visited the Stoke Newington mansion of John Dudley, a relative of the Queen's favourite, the Earl of Leicester. (*CM*)

Although some of the nineteenth-century houses have gone, Queen Elizabeth's Walk appears to retain some of its character as a quiet residential street. What is not obvious from this picture is that it sits next to the Lordship South estate, one of Stoke Newington Borough Council's housing developments of the interwar years. This is another example of middle- and working-class housing found close together. (*DM*)

An idyllic view of 1882 shows Paradise Row, the Georgian houses at the west end of Stoke Newington Church Street. In the early nineteenth century they accommodated members of the Quaker banking Hoare family, prominent in the campaign against slavery. Paradise Row is reflected in the New River, a water course constructed in the early seventeenth century to provide clean water for London from Ware in Hertfordshire. (*HAD*)

Some of the Georgian houses of Paradise Row still survive, but this stretch of the New River was filled in the 1950s. A dip along the edge of Clissold Park marks where it ran. Clissold Park itself was saved from development by the first of Stoke Newington's amenity campaigns in 1887, and opened to the public in 1889. It is still as heavily used by local residents as its Victorian saviours intended. (*DM*)

The northern side of Stoke Newington Church Street, opposite the site of the new St Mary's church, is occupied by Church Row in this view of 1880. Church Row was a handsome terrace of early eighteenth-century houses on the site of Stoke Newington manor house, the residence of John Dudley. (*AB*)

Stoke Newington Borough Council demolished Church Row in 1935 to build its new town hall, designed by Reginald Truelove. Since 1965 the town hall, redesignated as municipal offices, has housed a range of Hackney Council services. With much of the building currently empty, it faces an uncertain future. (*DM*)

Clapton Common Road, *c.* 1870, just short of the junction with Stamford Hill. The chain fence on the right is the new surround of Craven Pond, formerly Leg of Mutton Pond, which took its newer name from the nearby estate of one John Craven. In the centre is the brand new Amhurst Park next to Brinkburn, later no. 85 (and later still 115) Stamford Hill, typical of the spacious residences of the moneyed middle classes with which Stamford Hill was once lined. (*GJ*)

Between 1890 and the First World War the land around Stamford Hill was heavily built up, and Stamford Hill was commercialised to serve the new, lower middle-class population of the area. Brinkburn was demolished in 1912 to be replaced by a row of four shops called Market Parade. It appears that only the middle two, Lisa Star Nails and its southerly neighbour, are of the original 1912 building. Stamford Hill is the centre of London's Hassidic Jewish population, but Lisa's is a reminder that other communities, such as the African Caribbean community, make their home here as well. (*DM*)

Egerton Road was laid out in 1873. In this leafy view of 1900 it is dominated by the Agapemonite church, the magnificent place of worship erected in 1892–5 for the Agapemone sect. Visible, black against the spire, are A.G. Walter's sculptures of the Four Winged Beasts of the Evangelists – a man for St Matthew, a lion for St Mark, a bull for St Luke and an eagle for St John. (*HAD*) *Inset*: The modern Egerton Road is dominated by the New Synagogue. This was built for an Ashkenazi Jewish congregation in 1913–15 to a design that resembled their former place of worship at Great St Helens in the City of London. In 1987 the New Synagogue was sold to a Hassidic congregation. The Agapemonite church survives as the Church of the Good Shepherd, and preserves the most important – and atmospheric – church interior in Hackney. (*DM*)

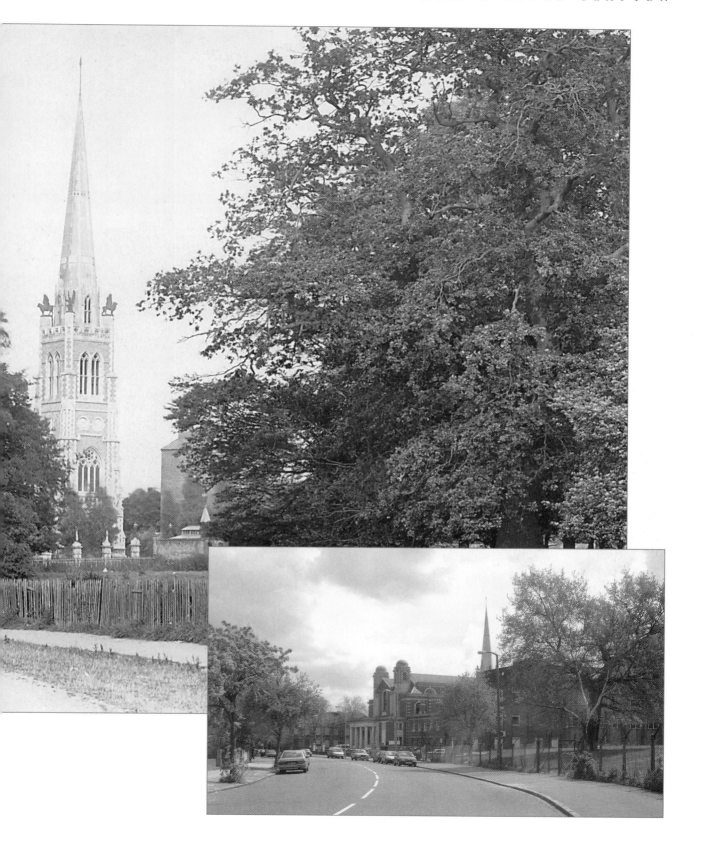

Buccleuch Terrace, built on the north side of Clapton Common in about 1825, contained 'lofty and well-proportioned drawing rooms, opening by French casements to iron balconies'. But it was rather less grand than the estate agents and this view from about 1900 suggest. Local historian Florence Bagust recorded that in each house 'the basement is large and gloomy, the stairs high and many, and there is no bathroom'. Soon after the terrace was built one of the central houses collapsed because it was so shoddily constructed. (*HAD*)

By the time Bagust wrote in the 1930s the whole of the terrace had been abandoned by the upper middle classes, for whom it had been built, and the houses were in multi-occupancy. Hackney Council started demolishing the terrace before the Second World War, and by 1951 had built a block of self-contained 'bed-sitting-room flats for single women' already resident in the borough, the first in London. So well regarded was this development that at least one young woman from outside the borough tried to persuade a Hackney friend to apply for a flat on her behalf using her own name! (*MK*)

This view of the west side of Clapton Common in 1885 shows the distinguished late eighteenth-century Clapton Terrace. To the south is St Thomas's church, built in about 1774; its tower was added in 1829. This was one of the wealthiest areas of Hackney in the 1880s. (*AB*)

Clapton Terrace and the tower of St Thomas's church are remarkable survivors. The body of St Thomas's was rebuilt after war damage in 1940. The Broad Common Estate beyond it had been built by 1960. (*DM*)

Oldhill Street was developed in the late eighteenth century to accommodate those with enough money to live in the clean air of Upper Clapton, but not enough money to be able to afford one of the grand houses in Clapton Terrace. In this picture of about 1885 Snewin's Dairy occupies the premises on the right. (*AB*)

Oldhill Street is now devoid of either interest or charm. The modern shops at the front of Feldman Close on the right conceal Tyssen Primary School which was built in 1938. (*DM*)

Spring Hill looking west, 1901. The grounds that would become Springfield Park are on the left and the playing fields, with cricket pavilion and tennis courts are the right. Behind is High Bridge, dating from the late eighteenth century, when it replaced the ferry across the Lea. (*GJ*)

The thatched cottage has given way to Lingwood Road, laid out in 1908, but the playing fields and pitches still survive. Springfield Park was laid out in 1905, incorporating the grounds of large houses (one of which survives in the park) and Spring Hill Farm, which saved the entire area giving way to Edwardian streets. (*DM*)

Just south of High Bridge was Horse Shoe Point and Willow Field Cottage, photographed in 1901 from the Walthamstow side. In the *Hackney Street Directory* of 1845 it was the riverside residence of James Burch. However, while filter beds and sewers in Hackney had solved the clean water problem for the borough by 1901, the river remained heavily polluted, as both Walthamstow and Leyton still poured untreated sewage into it. (*HAD*)

It is still one of the most picturesque parts of the borough and well visited by river walkers, visitors to Springfield Park and canal users. Many barges line this part of the river with the large marina on the Walthamstow side. The number of bridges on this stretch allows walkers freedom to enjoy both sides of the river. (*DM*)

This view from the Walthamstow side of the river looks towards the Anchor and Hope and Beehive public houses. Along with a third pub, the Robin Hood, just off picture on the right, this made a lively stretch of the river. They fronted the small settlement of cottages and lanes that made up the Bakers Hill, Little Hill and Big Hill area. With High Bridge to the north and Middlesex Wharf to the south, these riverside settlements and their associated economic activities, were well established by the early nineteenth century, with the ferries, isolated houses and an inn recorded in 1725. Rowing and pleasure boating were at their most popular during the 1860s, although many clubs were short-lived as they were based on seasonal income. Interest had declined by 1900, with many clubs having gone out of business. The boat club at High Hill Ferry, however, thrives to this day. (*AB*)

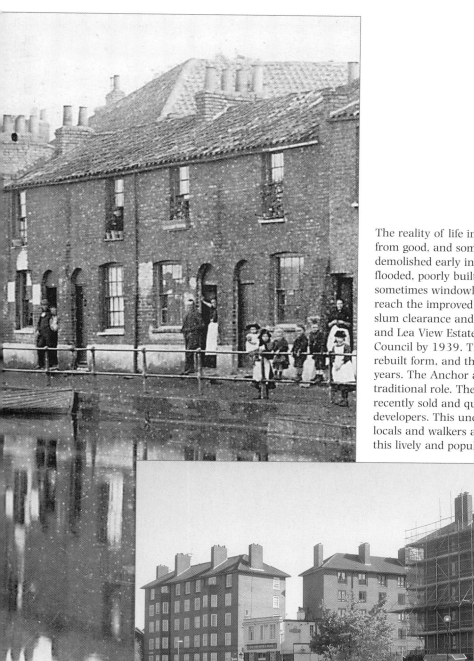

The reality of life in these picturesque settlements was far from good, and some of the most unhealthy cottages were demolished early in the twentieth century. Regularly flooded, poorly built and maintained, cramped and sometimes windowless, many of these buildings did not reach the improved standards of the 1930s. Following the slum clearance and rehousing programmes, all were gone and Lea View Estate had been built by the London County Council by 1939. The two pubs have survived, albeit in rebuilt form, and the Beehive without a licence for some years. The Anchor and Hope, as seen, maintains its traditional role. The other pub, the Robin Hood was recently sold and quickly demolished by private housing developers. This understandably caused outrage among locals and walkers alike, who had continued to patronise this lively and popular pub. (*MK*)

Nos 103–15 Upper Clapton Road, *c.* 1890. Shop fronts have been added to what are probably early nineteenth-century houses, either side of the Rossington Street junction. F. Brown's was a florist's shop, and the policeman, the errand boy and their companions are standing in front of the garden of the Willows, residence of one Robert Ford. (*AB*)

This stretch of Upper Clapton Road is unusual in that so many of the original buildings survive. Elsewhere in this area many of the Victorian buildings have been replaced by public housing, either as part of slum-clearance programmes, such as happened to Conduit Place, Rossington Street, or because they were too large for twentieth-century living, as was the case with Buccleuch Terrace. (*DM*)

Another photograph from about 1890, this time of Northwold Road, and once again an appreciative audience has assembled to watch and be photographed. The public house in the middle is the Red Lion, of which William Farmer was the landlord. (*AB*)

Beyond the scaffolding on the right in this modern view of Northwold Road is Clapton Library, opened by the Metropolitan Borough of Hackney in 1914. It was externally refurbished in 1998. As elsewhere, Hackney's older libraries have been an increasing challenge for the borough to maintain. They have been moving with the times however, and the computer and internet service introduced in the mid-1990s is popular and well used. (*DM*)

This view of about 1900 looks west along Brooke Road towards the junction with Darville Road. The green space on the right is the southern end of Stoke Newington Common, an open space misnamed as it has never been within the administrative boundaries of Stoke Newington. (*HAD*)

Although flats have been built on the right, Brooke Road remains typical of this part of Hackney, in which relatively few modern developments interrupt the rows of Victorian houses. (*DM*)

The Great Eastern Railway opened its station at Clapton in 1873 on the new branch to Chingford. It is on the extreme left of this photograph from about 1887. The houses next to it are rather older; they are Myrtle Cottage and Vine Cottage, and the premises of Snewin's decorators and undertakers. (*AB*)

Gunton Road, on the right, was laid out in 1887, and the process is clearly shown in the early picture. It is a shame that Clapton station is now so run down, as relatively few of Hackney's dozen Victorian stations still survive. (*DM*)

The Jolly Anglers public house, Middlesex Wharf, 1884, at the end of a row of cottages, stables and sheds that ran north from Lea Bridge. Posing for the photograph are F.H. Fullcher, his men and boats. In a sale notice of 1846 the Jolly Anglers is described as containing a handsome tea room with two fireplaces, three bedrooms, a small dining room, a bar and bar parlour, a tap room, kitchen and cellar. The area was prone to flooding, as the Lea frequently broke its banks, putting North Millfields underwater. (*AB*)

Middlesex Wharf did not survive the rigorous public-health measures of the local authorities, and was slum-cleared during the 1930s. It is now a riverside walk. Latham's woodyard is in the background, a lone survivor of the area's light industry and wharves. Through the gap is Riverside Close, a housing scheme of the 1980s, when derelict sites were developed and the river walk improved, now with established gardens and trees. (*MK*)

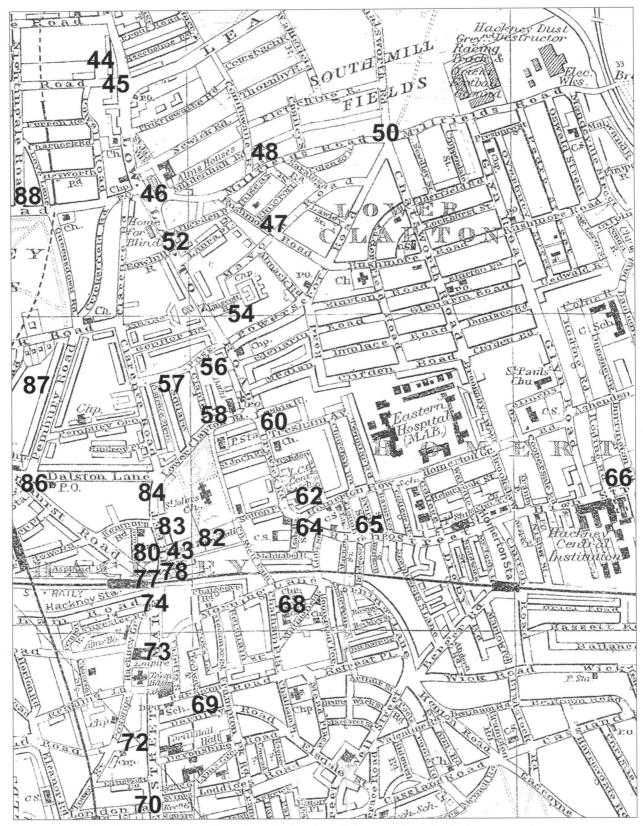

Map 2: Central Hackney, *c.* 1935. Numbers show the location of photographs and refer to page numbers.

42

Lower Clapton, Homerton & Central Hackney

Montage of the Old Town Hall, *c.* 1870 (*HAD*) and HSBC, 2001. (*MK*)

This village scene, *c.* 1870, of the east side of Upper Clapton Road at the junction with Lea Bridge Road, was to last another ten years before clearance for Victorian shops and terraces. The busy crossroads with Lower Clapton and Kenninghall Roads lasted until the 1960s when the area was redeveloped for the building of the Lea Bridge roundabout, with substantial clearance on all four corners of the junction. (*GJ*)

The scheme was completed in 1972. The subways proved to be dank and at times dangerous places, and with locals preferring to chance it and cross the roads, they were closed in the mid-1990s. As lights returned to regulate traffic and pedestrians the whole purpose of the roundabout was gone; particularly so as dual-carriageways off the roundabout were never built, fortunately. (*MK*)

Before the 1880s the corner of Lower Clapton and Lea Bridge Roads was mainly the grounds of large eighteenth-century houses. It was always an important and busy transport route with north/south traffic through Clapton and as the main road crossing for the Lea. Complete with shops, banks, drinking fountains and public conveniences it was an important centre as well as a junction. (*HAD*)

Now as a centre for local Muslims to worship, the mosque has helped to preserve the people presence, so much wiped out by the removal of so many buildings and shops. The new mosque was opened in 1991. Other mosques in Hackney include the conversions of the old Apollo cinema and old Stoke Newington synagogue (in Dalston), and the new mosque in Kingsland Road. (*MK*)

Dating from the early nineteenth century, St James' Terrace ran from Pond House to Bow House and Pond Lane. At the time of this view, in about 1885, the rest of the east side of Clapton Pond up to Lea Bridge Road was made up of early eighteenth-century houses and grounds, including the Elms and Clapton House. However, Lower Clapton had seen building development since the 1860s, and change was sweeping in from the south. (*AB*)

Only two houses survived the building of Mildenhall Road in 1890 that cut the terrace in two. The southern end survived until the 1920s when it was demolished to make way for the public conveniences between Mildenhall and Millfields Roads. Pond House and the Bishops Wood Almshouses also survive today, but all the rest on the east side of the pond were cleared during the 1880s for the building of Newick and Thistlewaite Roads. (*MK*)

This view looks north-east to the last surviving stretch of Pond Lane Path in 1888, with the spire of the Clapton Wesleyan church and the trees and chimneys around Clapton Pond just visible. Pond Farm Nursery, on the right, survived into the early years of the twentieth century, albeit in a reduced form. The path originally ran south-east to Chatsworth Road (itself a path from Homerton through the fields to Lea Bridge). (*AB*)

The building of Rushmore Road was completed by 1890 and Millfields School (just out of the picture on the right) was opened by the London Schools Board in 1895 and continues as a mixed primary school today. Victorian terraces survive alongside new housing in the 1980s on the left. (*MK*)

Main picture: At the southern end of the pond and St James Terrace was the entrance to Pond Lane, now Millfields Road, seen here in 1879. A little way down the lane, this view is taken from the edge of Pond Farm with front gardens visible on the right. The lane then became a muddy farm track, winding down the hill to a footbridge over the canal, called the Cow Bridge. (*AB*)

Bottom left: This 1905 view shows Millfields Road, laid out in 1880, following the route of the path from the junction with Saratoga Road down to Chatsworth Road. Not all the land was built on, and the Mill Fields survived as Millfields Park and playing fields. (*HAD*)

Bottom right: Much of the Victorian street remains. On the left is Pond Farm Estate, built following bombing in 1941. Lower Clapton was peppered with bombs during the blitz, and the area has similar small housing developments, and 'in-fills' in terraces. Beyond Chatsworth Road, on the last stretch of the original path, for much of the twentieth century familiar features were the Clapton Stadium, home of Clapton (later Leyton) Orient, and a power station by the Cow Bridge. Later a dog track, the stadium had given way to housing by 1980. (*MK*)

The shop of newsagent H.S. Francis, from an undated postcard donated to Hackney Archives. It turned out to be 185 Powerscroft Road on the corner with Millfields Road, found in a 1912 *Kelly's Local Street and Trade Directory*. The shop front displays the advertising and names of its time, with some surviving to this day; thankfully some products, processes and substances have not. (*HAD*)

Bhupendra and Kokila Patel and their son recreate the scene. The shop itself was totally rebuilt, having collapsed dramatically in 1987 in an incident the Patel family will not forget. The *Hackney Gazette* ran the story on the front page with the headlines 'Family Cheat Death as House Collapses' and 'Lucky to be Alive'. The sensational headlines were not without reason. The family also owned the house next door, which had access to the shop. Builders, carrying out structural work to the shop, had finished for the day, but Bhupendra and his son were still in the shop. First they heard creaking and then plaster began to fall from the ceiling. They ran through the door into the house as the shop collapsed around them into a pile of rubble. Both escaped with cuts and bruises. The shop was rebuilt and reopened seven months later. (*MK*)

Main picture: Lower Clapton Road, *c.* 1905, looking north from the junction with Atherton Road on the right, to the spire of the Clapton Wesleyan church. From the left is a line of early eighteenth-century houses, the British Asylum for Deaf and Dumb Females (nicknamed 'Piss-pot Hall' because of the large urns on the gate posts), the Gavillers family home and Byland House, the former home of local landowners the Powell family, close relatives of Robert Baden-Powell, founder of the Scouts. (*CM*)

Bottom left: By 1932 all the houses were empty, neglected and some damaged by fire. Despite some local protests they were demolished to make way for Powell House, with 198 flats for 900 people, which opened in 1934. This view was taken a year later in 1935. However, the building suffered from poor design and structural defects, and in later years it was very unpopular. It was demolished in the early 1980s as it was beyond economic repair. (*HAD*)

Bottom right: Houses with front gardens and small blocks of flats that recall early nineteenth-century townhouses now line the street. The front gardens and trees provide the finish to the improved streetscape. The Clapton Wesleyan church faced declining numbers by the early 1930s and closed in 1934. Demolished shortly after the Powell House photograph, the congregation continued in the old school on Downs Road, which is still a place of worship today. The tower block in the distance is the 1960s Gooch House at the Lea Bridge Roundabout. (*MK*)

Congress Hall, *c.* 1905. This was originally the London Orphan Asylum, built in 1825 with substantial grounds and gardens to the front on Lower Clapton Road. From the 1860s these gardens gave way to Victorian streets, and in 1882 the building became the London headquarters of the Salvation Army. (*HAD*)

Top: Congress Hall survived the Second World War, but it was a close shave. This powerful image from the morning of 16 October 1940 shows its unscathed columns and pediment as backdrop to the destruction of Linscott Road and bewildered local people. (*HAD*)

Above: When the Salvation Army left in the 1970s, most of the building, except the portico and flanking columns, were sadly demolished for extensions to Clapton Girls' school on Laura Place. Flats replaced the destroyed houses on the right, and the site of the end of Mayola Road on the left was included in the school extensions. This striking reminder of the past often takes newcomers by surprise, tucked away on an ordinary London side street. The Hackney Historic Buildings Trust is seeking funding and a secure future for the building; a recent neon light installation on the Portico states optimistically 'Everything Is Going To Be Alright'. (*MK*)

This house on Lower Clapton Road, seen in about 1880, was the residence of Dr Joseph Priestley from 1792 to 1794, when he preached at the Gravel Pit chapel on Chatham Place. During the 1870s the house was used as a school. By the lamp-post is the entrance to Clapton Passage. (*HAD*)

The house was demolished and this stretch of the road was rebuilt in about 1883. The Victorian urban model of shops with dwellings above on a busy main road has survived intact. A plaque commemorates Priestley on the Pancho Villa Tex Mex Canteena. (*MK*)

Clapton Square was laid out in 1816 on The Field, an area bordered with roads and paths, and the houses in this 1879 view of the west and north sides date from then. Some houses in the north-east corner dated from the previous century, but were cleared by 1901 to build Cavendish and St John's Mansions. (*AB*)

All in view have survived, but other parts of square have not, mainly because of bomb damage in the Second World War. All of the east side was cleared by 1947 and has since been the site of a small social services building, now sold to developers. The council and the local conservation group are currently considering an application to return that side of the square to residential use. (*MK*)

This is the last section of Lower Clapton Road where it turns to the west towards Clapton Square and Mare Street in 1884. Called Portland Place at the time, on the right is the entrance to the Portland Arms public house and a yard leading to a forge and stables. (*AB*)

Top: By 1905 the far terrace has acquired shop fronts and Kings Hall and the Elephants Head public house had replaced the shops, Portland Arms and forge in 1897. A horse-drawn tram completes the Edwardian street scene. (*AB*)

Above: When Lower Clapton Road was widened in the 1960s the houses opposite lost most of their front gardens, but otherwise all remains the same. Kings Hall survives with swimming pools, sauna, sports hall and children's playgroup; one of its original functions, to provide public washrooms, is no longer needed. Beyond Kings Hall some of the small shops still have rounded back rooms, features surviving from their time as the houses on Portland Place. The no. 38 bus completes the early twenty-first-century Hackney street scene. (*MK*)

Urswick Road looking north from College (Tresham) Avenue, *c.* 1880. Drayton House was one of the surviving pair of the Five Houses, the other is in the background behind the stable blocks that fronted on to the road. Dating from the eighteenth century, the Five Houses were next to the grounds of Hackney House. They acquired extra land when the house was demolished and the estate broken up in about 1800. Tresham Avenue is the site of the original drive to Hackney House, built in 1732, situated on the current junction of Blurton and Elderfield Roads. The Five Houses ran from Drayton House north along Lower Clapton Road to where the Round chapel is now. No longer used as residences, these large houses were easy prey for developers and were demolished in the 1880s. Ironically, the last occupants of Drayton House were C.E. Hilton Estate Agents. (*AB*)

In 1861, the estates to the east of Lower Clapton Road were acquired for development by the London and Surburban Land and Property Co. Standard late Victorian shops to the front, and terraces on Tresham Avenue and Lesbia Road, replaced the last two of the Five Houses in 1885; the other houses to the north were demolished to build Median and Glenarm Roads in 1867. Lesbia Road was built on the site of the stables between the two houses. But by the 1970s, with many properties dilapidated and still without basic services, the area from Median Road to Homerton Row was cleared. This unfortunately included early nineteenth-century stable buildings on Tresham Avenue, but it did uncover vaults of an old house and allow a full archaeological survey. The Lower Clapton Health Centre is now on the site of Drayton House and Lesbia Road, and the streets behind were replaced by the Jack Dunning Estate. (*MK*)

Right: Homerton Row looking east from the Urswick Road, *c.* 1886. The Board School is just out of the picture on the right and demolition of part of Alderman's Row for the building of Halidon Street is on the left. Further down Homerton Row was the City of London Workhouse, and by the 1890s the East London Fever Hospital. (*AB*)

Below: The building centre right, in this picture from 1969, survived the late Victorian redevelopment, but the rebuilt Homerton school on the right was a sign of change to come. Further down Homerton Row the Homerton Hospital, which opened in 1986, replaced the old Eastern Hospital. (*AW*)

Bottom right: The demolition of these streets at a time when conservation battles had been won elsewhere in Hackney was, looking back, controversial, but also indicative of the socio-economic make-up of the area in the 1970s. Property values and owner-occupation were low, the conditions of the houses poor and refurbishment more expensive than rebuilding. Many people lived in below-standard conditions. Jack Dunning Estate is one of the first 'lessons of the 1960s learned' developments of houses, small blocks and terraces, gardens, brick built; while uniform, it is broadly in keeping with the style of the area. Homerton Row has seen many changes, but not all the past was obliterated; the entrance to Halidon Road survives in the pavement, as does the original course of Homerton Row and its 'lane'-like quality, as it was never widened during any of the redevelopments. (*MK*)

This view looks straight down Homerton High Street from the junction with Homerton Row and Urswick Road, with a row of shops and the Peacock public house on the left. The yard of general contractor G. Moore and adjoining buildings were to give way in the late 1890s to shops and further building on Isabella Road. (*AB*)

With all of the south side swept away during the late twentieth century, the street has changed dramatically. Widened and now a busy main road, the Marion Court Estate is in the centre and to the right a modern Housing Association block of flats. The only surviving feature from the nineteenth century is the steps down to Link Street beyond the new block. (*MK*)

These late medieval timber-framed buildings in Homerton High Street were well recorded by artists and photographers, and were recognised as significant. However, they were in poor condition by this time, and had been demolished by 1887. The public house at the end, the Plough, was twice rebuilt in the nineteenth century. (*HAD*)

The Plough and the shops and houses that replaced the range have survived, while all else around has vanished, strangely recreating the site's separateness. Slum clearance, bomb damage and road widening have all played a part in shaping the modern street, now mainly a through-road rather than a high street, and without a unifying character. (*MK*)

At the east end of Homerton High Street, in 1885, settlement became countryside, and Marsh Hill was a lane leading down to the marshes mainly used by cattle going to graze. The old Marsh House was rumoured to have been used by Dick Turpin, and although there is no evidence to support this, the chance of getting mugged when crossing the marshes (or going anywhere at night) would have been quite high. The house itself is recorded on the Roque map of 1745, and is seen here on the corner with Wick Lane, later Sidney Street and now Kenworthy Road. (*AB*)

Marsh House was demolished in 1897 and the Victorian buildings that replaced it have come and gone. On the corner now is the Herbert Butler Estate, with Chevet and Mabley Street to the south. Although widened, Marsh Hill still retains its character in the way it weaves down to the marshes. On the north side we have surviving Victorian shops with Kingsmead Estate looming above. It was born out of controversy, when in the late 1930s, and despite howls of protest, the London County Council built on the marshes. In its defence, it stated that there was a housing shortage, many people still lived in slums, and anyway it was only a small site between the canal wharf and other housing. Kingsmead has seen the best and worst of times, but is currently undergoing major renovation work. (*MK*)

This is the Old Gravel Pit chapel, on Chatham Place in 1884. A century earlier it had been an independent meeting house where Unitarian thinkers, Richard Price and Joseph Priestley, were ministers (1792–3). The chapel was abandoned by the Unitarians in 1809 because it was unsafe. It was repaired and enlarged in 1853 for Congregational worshippers, who later moved to the Round chapel on Lower Clapton Road. (*AB*)

This building subsequently served as a mission and a Sunday School, and is now in industrial use. Extended to the road, the original building sits behind and a GLC plaque on the wall, facing Morning Lane, commemorates Priestley. In this view, it's school pick-up time at Morningside Primary School just next door. (*MK*)

Hackney Infant School, seen here in 1872, was built in 1859 to house the youngest pupils of the Hackney Free and Parochial Schools. It stood on part of the site of the famous plant nursery run by the Loddiges family, which between 1775 and 1854 specialised in exotic blooms grown in massive glasshouses. (*GJ*)

Hackney Free and Parochial School can trace its history back at least to 1580, when Elizabethan benefactors sought to give the children of Hackney the benefits of education. The modern secondary school was opened on the site of the old infants' school in 1952. (*MK*)

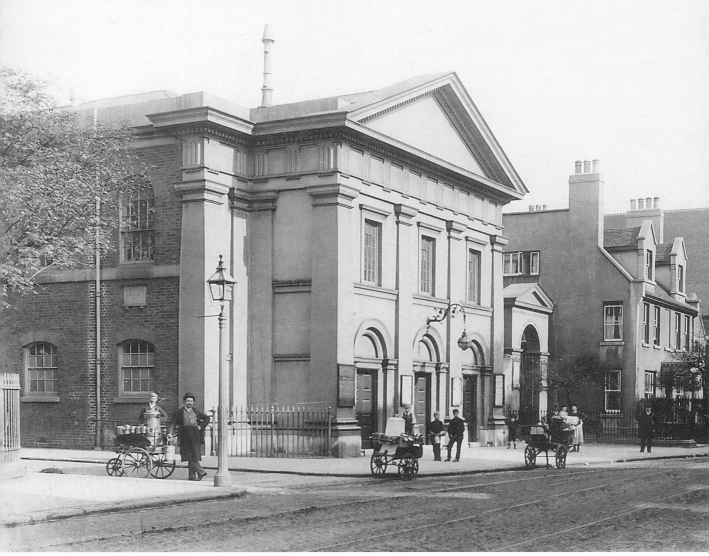

Above: An independent congregation dating from 1694 founded St Thomas' Square chapel in 1773. Unusually for a nonconformist place of worship it had its own graveyard, entered through the pedimented arch in the right centre of this 1886 view. Beyond the arch, and the house to the south of it, can be seen the Catholic Apostolic church of 1874. (*AB*)

Opposite, top: In 1912 the chapel had become the Empress cinema. The film showing is Edwin S. Porter's *Tessibel of the Storm Country* of 1914, starring America's Sweetheart, Mary Pickford. The building was substantially rebuilt and later served as a bingo hall, until demolition in the late 1980s. (*HAD*)

Opposite, bottom: The building on the site of St Thomas' Square chapel is the hall of residence for Cordwainers College, a school for designers of leather goods, now merged with the London College of Fashion. The college itself occupies the former buildings of the Lady Holles school to the south of the former Catholic Apostolic, now Greek Orthodox church. The archway still leads to the former chapel graveyard, now a recreation ground, though with some surviving memorials. (*MK*)

Mare Street, *c*. 1872, looking north from the junction with Richmond Road. The grand houses on the left were to survive well into the 1960s for industrial use. Centre right is the second Hackney Town Hall, built in 1866 on a site in front of the current town hall. (*GJ*)

The Richmond Road junction is now choked with traffic, and certainly with fewer trees than in 1872. In 2000 there was some local controversy about the removal of trees in front of the Ocean music venue, formerly the library, the domed building on the right-hand side of the road. Coincidentally, the nineteenth-century historian of Hackney, Benjamin Clarke, complained angrily about the local authority removing trees in Mare Street over a century before. (*MK*)

Local photographer George James took this view of the east side of Mare Street in about 1870 when it still had its eighteenth-century profile. This vanished between 1877 and 1879 when the Metropolitan Board of Works, the London-wide planning authority of the time, widened the street to accommodate increased traffic. (*GJ*)

The widened Mare Street was lined with late nineteenth-century, purpose-built, commercial premises, many of which survive. The northern stretch of the east side was rebuilt several times, and the 1908 development survives today. (*MK*)

The North London Railway came to Hackney in 1850, the bridge over Mare Street dominating the ancient centre of the village. That village past is still evident however in the Old King's Head public house, perhaps a sixteenth-century building, on the right of this view of about 1870. (*GJ*)

The King's Head had been rebuilt in 1878, and this view of 1887 shows a Mare Street far more commercialised than had been the case in the 1870s. The bulk of Matthew Rose's department store now looms above the railway bridge in the background. (*HAD*)

The east side of Mare Street was comprehensively rebuilt in 1908, two years before this view was taken. Tram lines are visible in the road, and three tramcars are emerging from under the railway bridge, partly hidden by the wagon in the middle of the road. Rising beyond the bridge is St Augustine's tower, now visible because of the road widening. On the left, next to the bridge, are the premises of the Hackney Furnishing Co. Ltd, a building which from its appearance in the previous two pictures probably dated from the late seventeenth or early eighteenth century. (*HAD*)

War and redevelopment resulted in some changes, but much of the east side remains as it did in 1910. Woolworths rebuilt their store in 1935 and the railway bridge was replaced in 1973, with passenger services recommencing on the North London Line in 1985. Throughout, Mare Street has maintained its department stores and variety of small local businesses; it is still one of the borough's major shopping centres. (*MK*)

These buildings stood on the corner of Mare Street and Amhurst Road, and this view dates from 1873. P.G. Winny's haberdashers shop is in the centre. The corner was totally rebuilt in 1881, with a new public house on the site, the Railway Tavern. (*GJ*)

The Railway Tavern was rebuilt in 1955 following bomb damage during the Second World War. On the east side of Mare Street is the old town hall, now the now a branch of HSBC. The building has been refaced but is still basically the one that was built in 1802 (and later extended) to house Hackney's parish government. (*MK*)

This view south down Mare Street to the railway bridge dates from about 1870. It shows the edge of the first Hackney station of the North London Railway, opened by 1850 on the east side of Mare Street. The Eight Bells public house on the left was demolished in about 1880. (*GJ*)

By the time this picture was taken in 1884 the Railway Coal Depot occupied the site of the earlier station, together with a handsome signal box. The railway station had been moved in 1870 to the site of the present Hackney Central station. (*AB*)

This part of Mare Street was very badly damaged by a bomb on the night of 19/20 March 1941. The area between St Augustine's Tower and the railway bridge was almost completely flattened, the old town hall remarkably surviving. The row of flat-roofed shops, including an estate agent's and a hardware shop, date from 1959. (*MK*)

Above: This part of Mare Street was called Church Street until 1869. Now known as the Narroway, in 1872 much of it was lined with eighteenth-century houses. The block on the left housed Matthew Rose's drapery after 1852. (*GJ*)

Opposite, top: Following the widening of Mare Street, Rose's took the opportunity to expand their operations and developed this sizeable department store. The firm described itself as a general drapers and complete house furnishers, and lasted until 1936. (*AB*)

Opposite, bottom: This branch of Marks and Spencer was built in 1936, but the buildings to the north of it survive from the 1908 photograph. Mare Street has retained its commercial character, although given the presence of McDonald's and Marks and Spencer at street level this could be any High Street in Great Britain. The facsimile gaslamp echoes its Victorian predecessor. (*MK*)

All that remained of Hackney's medieval church in 1885 was the tower, now known as St Augustine's Tower, and the mausoleum of the Rowe family to the west of it. The new church of St John at Hackney had been built to meet the demands of a growing population between 1791 and 1797. (*AB*)

The Rowe chapel was demolished in 1896 after it had become unsafe. At the same time many of the gravestones were resited along the walls of the churchyard and paths were laid out to create a recreation ground. Today it provides a leafy refuge from the fumes of Mare Street for Hackney people. (*MK*)

Another of George James' shots of Mare Street, *c.* 1870 shows no. 387, with first-floor windows in arched recesses and a prominent porch. It was the Manor House, home in the mid-nineteenth century of J.R.D. Tyssen, a local antiquarian and brother of the lord of the manor. The house was on the site of the New Mermaid Tavern, that with its pleasure grounds and assembly rooms was the social centre of Hackney for many years. (*GJ*)

The Manor House is still a prominent building in the Narroway, occupied by Shoefayre on the ground floor. The assembly rooms behind it continued well into the nineteenth century as a venue for social and political meetings. The entrance is the prominent doorway beyond the porch of the Manor House above. Kenmure Road was laid out on the site in 1877. (*MK*)

At its northern end Mare Street meets Dalston Lane, Clarence Road, and Lower Clapton Road, seen here in 1876. For many years this road junction was known as Ward's Corner, after the early eighteenth-century MP and speculator John Ward, who owned a mansion on the site of the shops on the left. Ward's house survived in multi-occupancy until about 1847. The shops on the right were there in 1853. The majestic Prince of Wales public house dominates the Dalston Lane turning. Mr R. Pierpoints was the landlord. Facing down Mare Street, the white building with the pediment is Clarence House, which was built before 1831. (*GJ*)

Although the Prince of Wales has been demolished for the New Pembury Estate, many of the other buildings survive. On either side of the former Clarence House, Hackney Housing Advice Centre, 2 Clarence Road, to the left, and 1 Lower Clapton Road to the right are recognisably the same buildings as in 1876. Comparing these two views brings home the amount of street furniture, such as street lamps, litter bins and barriers, that we take for granted today. (*MK*)

Amhurst Road in 1880 was a main thoroughfare of the prosperous middle-class area around Hackney Downs. Congregationalists worshipped at the elaborate church on the corner of Amhurst Road and Pembury Road in the centre of the picture. It was designed in about 1863 by Henry Fuller to seat 1,000 worshippers. (*HAD*)

Dominating the modern view of the Amhurst Road and Pembury Road intersection is the huge Downs Court that replaced the congregational church in 1937. Built in a style of architecture more familiar from parts of London such as St John's Wood, it was a commercial rather than council development of one- and two-bedroom flats. Until recently this was one of the more run-down areas of Hackney, but with the conversion of the Technical College into flats, just out of shot, the tide of gentrification is beginning to rise over this corner of the borough. (*MK*)

Pembury Road was another of the middle-class housing developments in the area of Hackney Downs dating from 1865. The historian Benjamin Clarke recalled from his childhood that before the road was built the area was one of 'gravel pits and small bits of ponds, the abode of frogs . . . which met with scant mercy at our schoolboys' merciless hands'. (*AB*)

The houses along Pembury Road were the subject of compulsory purchase before the Second World War by the London County Council. Part of the estate was opened by 1938. Shortly before the demise of the Greater London Council, successor to the London County Council, the Pembury Estate was transferred to the London Borough of Hackney. In common with many of Hackney's estates it has now passed to a housing association, now the preferred means of delivering housing to those who cannot afford to buy their own. (*MK*)

The Downs Hotel was built in 1863, to provide the users of Hackney Downs with a place of refreshment. Among the social groups which met here was the Pickwick Bicycling Club founded there in 1870. Its numbers are limited to the number of characters in Dickens' *Pickwick Papers*, and it celebrated its 125th anniversary in 1995. The lane leading up the side of the hotel is now called Downs Lane, but was known as Love Lane until 1938. There is no evidence to connect this to Hackney Downs' reputation for courting couples and amorous encounters; a local minister, Mr Cross, complained, in letters to the *Hackney Gazette* in 1911, of couples rolling in the grass and of depraved behaviour! (*AB*)

The Downs Road area changed substantially in the late 1960s when the Greater London Council built the Nightingale Estate. This was a more than usually unpleasant concrete wasteland, although Downsview School, built next to the hotel, was admired at the time as 'visually interesting'. The Nightingale Estate is now being redeveloped, with only one of the original six tower blocks intended to remain, seen refurbished in this view. New housing is being built on cleared sites and the low-rise blocks are also being redeveloped; the long wall-like blocks are being broken up into smaller sections with new balconies, increased lighting and entry phones. The completed first phase is just visible on the right. (*MK*)

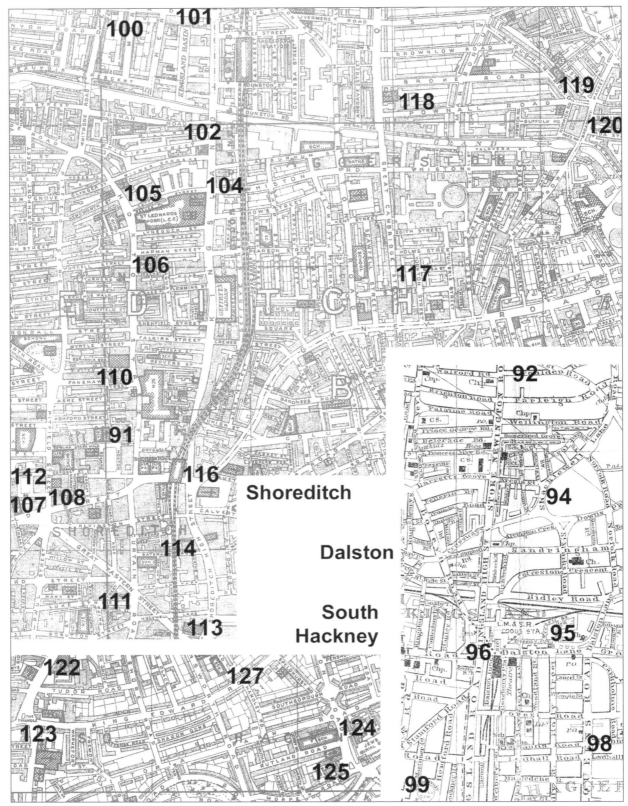

Map 3: Dalston, Shoreditch and South Hackney, *c.* 1935. Numbers show the location of photographs and refer to page numbers.

Dalston, Shoreditch & South Hackney

Montage of Hoxton Square, 1920 (*LMA*) and 2001. (*MK*)

The ancient parish of Hackney was split into three in 1825 becoming West, South and St John at Hackney. The local Anglican clergy were very keen to extend the influence of the Church of England in the parishes, and education was an important part of this programme. West Hackney National School was built in Evering Road in 1837 to serve West Hackney parish, national schools being the day schools of the Anglican Church. The school and some of its pupils are seen here in 1864, in one of the earliest surviving photographs of Hackney. (*HAD*)

West Hackney National School was extended in about 1873, and the central section is a remarkable survivor of the earliest days of educational provision in Hackney. It closed in 1906, but the building served as the west Hackney parish Sunday schools and as the Grange House recreation club. It is now in industrial use. (*DM*)

The village of Shacklewell grew up around its green in the sixteenth century, and despite the proximity of Stoke Newington Road, preserved a genteel remoteness from the rest of Hackney. The nineteenth-century composer Vincent Novello moved to Shacklewell Green in 1823, but soon moved away again because he thought the village was too secluded for his children to be educated. An impression of rural seclusion is still evident in this view of Shacklewell Green in May 1886. (*HAD*)

Shacklewell is now very much built up, and some of the eighteenth-century houses were cleared in 1936. Through the trees is Kingsland School, built as Dalston County Secondary School for Girls in 1937. It was named Kingsland School in 1982 when it was merged with two other secondary schools. (*DM*)

Dalston Lane is an ancient thoroughfare, linking the old village of Kingsland with that of Dalston, sited around the bend in the lane where the Three Compasses public house is. This is the western end in about 1905. The police station, seen here on the left, dates from 1872. (*HAD*)

The police station was rebuilt in 1914, but closed in the 1990s when policing was rationalised in Hackney. Opposite is a recent building built by the Peabody Trust that is totally out of keeping with the rest of Dalston Lane; it involved the demolition of houses from about 1816 with Victorian shop-fronts. Its chequered façade has given rise to a local nickname – the 'Battenberg building'! (*DM*)

95

The intersection known locally as Dalston Junction, after the nearby railway station, has a very long history. In medieval times a leper hospital was built on the corner of Balls Pond Road and Kingsland Road. It was not finally demolished until 1845. Sixty years later this view along Kingsland High Street shows as busy a shopping street as it is today. The chain stores were already beginning to advance – Boots the Chemist is the shop on the right with the single, large, pedimented second-floor window. (*HAD*)

Much of Kingsland High Street was rebuilt in the early twentieth century, such as the former Boots, which is now a fried chicken takeaway. Kingsland received an economic boost in the 1980s with the opening of Dalston Cross shopping centre and Dalston Kingsland station. Ridley Road street market, opposite the station, is a vibrant, ethnically diverse shopping experience in modern Kingsland. And it always was; mainly a Jewish food market in the 1930s, it now serves the local Afro-Caribbean, Asian, Turkish and Cockney communities with an atmosphere and range of food and goods found in only a few places in London. (*DM*)

Mapledene Road was laid out after 1839, when it was called Shrubland Grove. The developers were the Rhodes family, relatives of the Victorian imperialist Cecil Rhodes. Like much of the Rhodes' developments, Mapledene Road consists of short terraces and semi-detached villas for the prosperous middle classes. This view is from 1912. (*HAD*)

Unlike many of the developments intended to house the middle classes, Mapledene Road did not substantially decline in social terms over the nineteenth and twentieth centuries. In the early 1980s the future prime minister Tony Blair and his wife Cherie lived at no. 59, the house at the end of the little terrace of four on the left of this picture. (*MK*)

Another area built for the middle classes, but one that rapidly moved down market, was De Beauvoir Town, on the western edge of Hackney. St Peter's church was built here in 1840–1 by the Benyon family, owners and developers of the estate, to the design of W.C. Lockner. It is seen here in about 1867. (*GJ*)

The church has not substantially changed in the preceding 160 years, though the area around it has. The proximity to industrial areas along the Regent's Canal, and the remoteness from the West End, meant that De Beauvoir Town, as a middle-class enclave, never really took off until modern times, when the Benyon family's original intentions began to be realised. It still, however, preserves a social and ethnic mix. (*MK*)

This is De Beauvoir Road, at the southern end of the development, in 1912. These large houses were occupied by two or more families by the beginning of the twentieth century, and the nearby Kingsland Basin on the Regent's Canal meant that light industry developed in the area. (*HAD*)

In the 1960s the complete demolition of De Beauvoir Town, except the square and the church, was planned. A vociferous and effective local campaign led by the De Beauvoir Association ensured that only the most dilapidated, southern part of the estate was bulldozed. The resulting local authority De Beauvoir Estate provided spacious modern accommodation. (*MK*)

At the corner of Kingsland Road and Downham Road the London Fire Brigade built a fire station in 1897, only a few years before this photograph was taken. Beyond it is the Metropolitan Hospital, opened in 1886. (*HAD*)

The rebuilt Kingsland Fire Station was opened in 1977. The Metropolitan Hospital was closed to in-patients in the same year, and now survives as workshops and light industrial units. (*DM*)

Left: The Shoreditch Vestry, the local authority of the period, appointed Public Library Commissioners for Shoreditch in 1891. They opened Shoreditch's first public library in the former offices of the Independent Gas Co. in Kingsland Road a year later. Four years later it was extended through the generosity of the radical philanthropist J. Passmore Edwards. After the opening of a second library in Pitfield Street the Kingsland Road branch was known as Haggerston Library. By 1900, when this picture was taken, it had an average daily attendance of 1,540 people. (*HAD*)

Above: Shoreditch Vestry, later the Metropolitan Borough Council, constructed other libraries in the borough. This practice was continued in the first years of the London Borough of Hackney, created in 1965, and covering Shoreditch. After the opening of the Rose Lipman Library in nearby Downham Road, Haggerston Library was closed in 1975. It has been empty ever since and the fabric of the building was ruined by rain pouring in through the old roof. Schemes for building flats behind the restored façade never seem to materialise, and the building continues to deteriorate. It remains one of the borough's longest-standing buildings at risk. (*DM*)

St Columba's church in Kingsland Road, seen here in 1905, was one of the churches built by the Haggerston Church Scheme, a High Church project to spread the influence of the Church of England in this part of Shoreditch. It was built in 1867–71 by James Brooks, a Stoke Newington architect, who built other churches for the scheme, such as St Chad's, Dunloe Street, and St Michael's, Mark Street. (*HAD*)

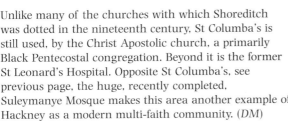

Unlike many of the churches with which Shoreditch was dotted in the nineteenth century, St Columba's is still used, by the Christ Apostolic church, a primarily Black Pentecostal congregation. Beyond it is the former St Leonard's Hospital. Opposite St Columba's, see previous page, the huge, recently completed, Suleymanye Mosque makes this area another example of Hackney as a modern multi-faith community. (*DM*)

Hoxton Street in 1910 was the busy centre of a teeming working-class area. A.S. Jasper, who published memoirs of his childhood in the Hoxton of the period, records barely imaginable deprivation going hand in hand with a remarkable zest for life. In the centre of the picture is Costers' Hall, the headquarters of the Costers' Mission that laid on services and social activities directed at the East End's costermongers. It was founded in 1861 by W.J. Orsman, a missionary and philanthropist known as 'the King of the Costers'. (*HAD*)

The buildings on either side of the Costers' Mission still survive, but the mission, renamed the Orsman Mission in memory of its founder, was rebuilt in 1955 after bomb damage. The former Admiral Keppel public house is now flats. The north end of Hoxton Street is now becoming an attractive place to live, benefiting from the artist's studios and new media companies of Hoxton Square further south. (*MK*)

On the left of this picture of Hoxton Street in 1910 are costers' barrows; itinerant traders mainly selling fruit and vegetables, with an individual culture nowadays as familiar as Pearly Kings and Queens. Over the road is the future of retailing – J. Sainsbury's! (*HAD*)

Sainsbury's future did not lie in Hoxton Street however, and the Halk Supermarket is more typical of the retail outlets of the area today. The building in the distance with the elaborate white stone details is part of the former Shoreditch workhouse, later St Leonard's Hospital. (*MK*)

Charles Square, *c.* 1900. The building with the elaborate doorway is no. 16, then the Shoreditch county court. It was subsequently, for many years, the regional Labour Party headquarters. It dates from about 1725 and is the only survivor of a period when Charles Square was the home of wealthy city merchants and professionals. (*HAD*)

Now, of course, Hoxton is becoming the home of wealthy city merchants again – or their twenty-first-century equivalents. This revival in Hoxton's fortunes is not too evident in this modern view, however. Charles Square remains quiet with other sides of the square replaced by public housing following slum clearance and bombing in the Second World War. (*MK*)

In 1683–4 Antony Ball and John Brown applied for a lease of what is now Hoxton Market, and for a licence to establish a twice-a-week food market in 1687–8. The scheme came to nothing, but the name stuck. By 1900 it was surrounded by bleak warehouses. The Hoxton Market Christian Mission offered a ray of hope, or at least a reliable source of food, to the deprived children who attended it. (*HAD*)

Top: A plaque from the mission, now in Hackney Museum – soon to reopen in the new Technology and Learning Centre (which will also include the borough's new central library and reference library) – next to Hackney Town Hall.

Above: The mission was established in Hoxton Market in 1886, and the premises seen here were rebuilt in 1904. The founders were the brothers John and Lewis Burtt, hence the Hoxton adage 'Daddy Burtt's for dinner'. Every child brought up in Hoxton before the war seems to remember the mission, and the story is told of children who started at the head of the dinner queue, ate up, and returned to the end of the queue for illicit seconds! Now the expensive loft spaces of Hoxton Market look down on a square where barefoot children once stood in line to receive free boots. (*MK*)

Another Hoxton legend was the Britannia Theatre, on Hoxton Street, opened in 1858, and the venue for elaborate pantomimes for over half a century. Seen here in 1890, it was still owned and run by the redoubtable Sara Lane, whose long and successful career awed even George Bernard Shaw. (*HAD*)

The Britannia's great days ended with Mrs Lane's death in 1899. The old theatre proved expensive to refurbish and was unsuccessful as a venue for variety. It became a cinema and was all but destroyed by a bomb in 1941. Only a brown heritage plaque on the modern flats indicates that this was once the site of a great theatre. (*DM*)

In 1897 Curtain Road was the centre of the furniture trade, Shoreditch's major employer. The splendid Victorian Gothic warehouses on the left suggest the care that nineteenth-century architects put into designing even industrial premises. Most of the furniture businesses were small operations in former residential properties, such as Barnett's on the right of the picture. (*HAD*)

J. Crispin and Sons, whose workshop is on the right, must be among the last surviving furniture-related companies in Shoreditch. The furniture industry declined as costs rose in the latter half of the twentieth century. The estate agent's in the restored Victorian warehouse is more indicative of the modern Shoreditch. (*DM*)

Pitfield Street also had businesses relating to furniture manufacturing, such as Green's timber yard on the left of this 1905 picture. Just visible on the left is the Shoreditch Library, part of a complex of library, baths and waste disposal plant opened by Shoreditch Vestry in 1899. (*HAD*)

Green's building still stands, as does the former library, which now houses studios and offices of the English National Opera. Despite popular legend, Pitfield Street takes its name from its seventeenth-century developer Sir Charles Pitfield, rather than a field with a pit for the burial of plague victims. (*DM*)

Great Eastern Street, *c.* 1900, when it was still a relatively new road, cut through by the Metropolitan Board of Works in 1876. The view is towards Shoreditch High Street with Fairchild Place running off to the right. The building with the four arches on the ground floor is the National Penny Bank, which was among the first enterprises opened in Great Eastern Street in 1878. (*HAD*)

Although most of the small businesses have gone, the buildings which housed them have survived. Great Eastern Street suffers as part of the Shoreditch one way system. Concern is being expressed that this part of Shoreditch is becoming the Soho of east London, such are the number of striptease joints and massage parlours. (*MK*)

This picture of Shoreditch High Street in 1905 shows a greater variety of businesses than are there today. From left to right are Saul Binderman's jewellers; Faith Brothers' hosiery; Eaton Buck & Son tailors, and further tailors and furniture-related trades, with the Bell Inn at the Rivington Street junction in the distance. Shoreditch High Street was one of the main fields of activity for the inventive pickpockets and petty thieves who infested the Old Nichol, the notorious slum behind Shoreditch church which was fictionalised as the 'Old Jago' in Arthur Morrison's 1897 novel *A Child of the Jago*. (*HAD*)

According to Arthur Harding, whose
memories of growing up in the Old Nichol
were recorded in the 1981 book *East End
Underworld*, Shoreditch High Street was the
main centre of amusement for the Nichol's
inhabitants. There were twenty-two pubs
between Shoreditch church and Liverpool
Street station. Whenever a shop fell vacant
itinerant showmen set up shows such as the
head-hunters of Borneo, two-headed ladies
and a donkey with its head where its tail
used to be! Many of the buildings remain
much the same above the ground floor. (*MK*)

This is the busy junction at Shoreditch church in about 1920. At the corner of Kingsland Road and Old Street is the Shoreditch station of the North London railway, opened in 1865, and rebuilt in 1927. The station was closed in 1941, some forty years before the railway line out of Broad Street closed in 1986. (*HAD*)

The 1927 station building now accommodates one of Shoreditch High Street's many footwear importing businesses. Beyond it is the 1930s half-timbered Spread Eagle public house. The railway bridge, which still carries the North London Railway track bed, is to be incorporated into the East London Line extension which is intended to link the City and Dalston once again. (*MK*)

When this photograph of the current Queensbridge Road was taken in about 1910, this, the Shoreditch end, was called Great Cambridge Street. On either side are more examples of early nineteenth-century middle-class houses, some of which still survive. The rather grim block, centre right, is St Saviour's Priory, a building of 1887, housing a community of Anglican nuns of the Society of St Margaret, founded in Haggerston in 1866. (*HAD*)

The modern view of Queensbridge Road is rather leafier, with Haggerston Park, developed over the site of bomb-damaged streets, on the left-hand side. St Saviour's Priory has been rebuilt, and still serves the parishes of Haggerston and Bethnal Green. In the distance is one of the surviving tower blocks of the notorious Holly Street Estate. (*MK*)

Pownall Road was laid out in the period after 1843 on the estate of Sir William Fowle Middleton, and named after his surveyor, George Pownall. The development of the Middleton estate was beset with difficulties, being too close to the canal and too far from a railway station to really attract commuters. By the time this photograph was taken in 1912, most of the houses would have been in multi-occupation, or used by light industrial enterprises. (*HAD*)

Much of the area between Shrubland Road and the Regent's Canal was redeveloped as public housing after 1960. On the south side of the modern Pownall Road is the Regent's Estate, a Greater London Council scheme of the 1970s. (*MK*)

Broadway Market, in 1905, offered a thriving street market to serve the surrounding busy working-class area, which dated from about 1871. The Lord Duncan, which dominates the right-hand side of the street, was built by 1865. Benjamin Clarke recalled that in the 1840s a shop here sold Hackney Buns, which apparently rivalled (and were presumably similar to) Chelsea Buns. (*HAD*)

In 1975 the London Borough of Hackney approved the Greater London Council's proposal to rehabilitate Broadway Market. The opposition argued that this discouraged any other investment in the area, and accelerated the blight. Today, however, Broadway Market grows increasingly prosperous, as new restaurants and refurbished pubs, such as the Dove on the extreme right, join that great survivor, Cooke's eel and pie shop. (*MK*)

This is one of the few photographs in this book from the 1930s. It shows Ada Street near Broadway Market. At the end of the street is the factory of W.J. Bush & Co., manufacturers of artificial flavourings. The photograph was taken prior to clearance as a slum, hence the house numbers written on the photograph. Ada Street had been built by 1851 and had been a poor area ever since. As seen earlier in the book, there were pockets of extreme poverty and slums across the borough. Larger slum areas included parts of Homerton, Morning Lane, Mare Street and nearly all of Shoreditch! (*HAD*)

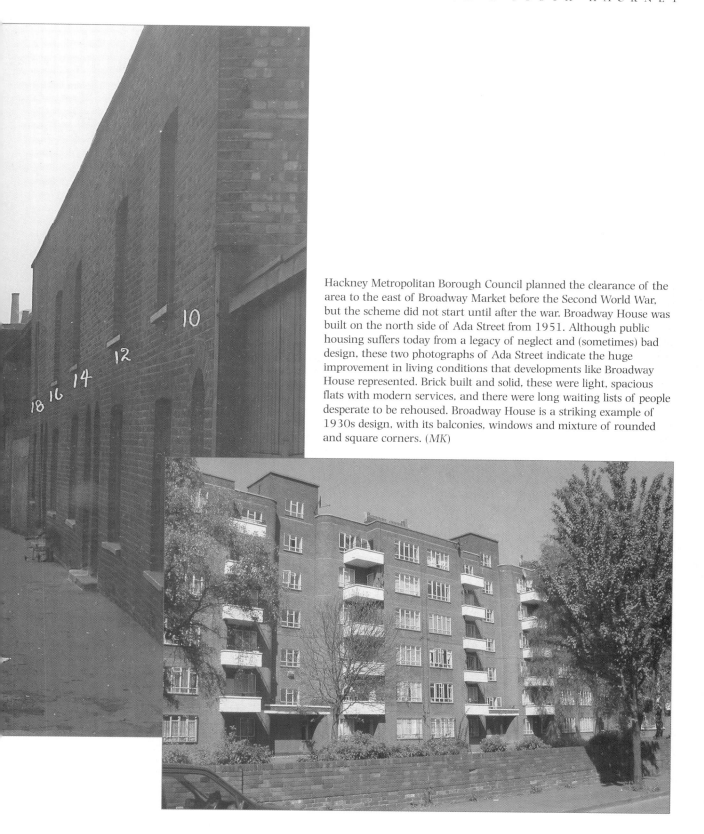

Hackney Metropolitan Borough Council planned the clearance of the area to the east of Broadway Market before the Second World War, but the scheme did not start until after the war. Broadway House was built on the north side of Ada Street from 1951. Although public housing suffers today from a legacy of neglect and (sometimes) bad design, these two photographs of Ada Street indicate the huge improvement in living conditions that developments like Broadway House represented. Brick built and solid, these were light, spacious flats with modern services, and there were long waiting lists of people desperate to be rehoused. Broadway House is a striking example of 1930s design, with its balconies, windows and mixture of rounded and square corners. (*MK*)

Well Street in 1874 had the air of the village street it had been for centuries, and this view from the junction with Mare Street had probably changed little in the previous fifty years. (*GJ*)

Well Street changed substantially in the years after 1874, and it continues to do so. On the right, flats are being built on the site of the former Regal/ABC cinema, and the street presents the usual modern jumble of street furniture. (*MK*)

This view of the Triangle, Mare Street, in about 1870, shows one of Hackney's first Roman Catholic churches, St John the Baptist. It was opened in 1848, having been designed by W.W. Wardell. Like many of the buildings around the Triangle it was destroyed by a V1 rocket on Saturday 12 July 1944. (*HAD*)

The destruction caused by the V1 is the reason for the undistinguished postwar buildings around the Triangle today. There were relatively few casualties given the scale of the incident – only two people were killed. The rebuilt St John's church is visible. It was built in 1956 and was remodelled in 1972. (*MK*)

The Jewish presence in South Hackney was very strong for much of the twentieth century, but was mostly gone by the 1980s. The Jewish cemetery in Lauriston Road was opened in 1788. (*GJ*)

The cemetery lodge survives, but the prayer hall has been demolished. The cemetery itself was closed in 1886 and is now maintained by the United Synagogue. (*MK*)

Lauriston Road used to be known as Grove Street, which wandered through the fields from Well Street towards Mile End. Once Victoria Park had been laid out, south Hackney became an increasingly attractive place to live. These houses at the junction with Morpeth Road were built in the 1870s. Through the trees rises the Swiss Cottage public house, and the road curves away past one of the lodges of Victoria Park. (*HAD*)

The Swiss Cottage was demolished after the war, and we can now see the Royal Inn on the Park beyond it. Lauriston Road has certainly come up in the world in the last five years. It now contains café-bars, designer clothes shops for adults and children, and that barometer of gentrification, a delicatessen. (*MK*)

125

South Hackney was built up from the 1840s, and King Edward Road was among the earliest streets in this area to be laid out. The road is named after Edward VI, benefactor of St Thomas' hospital on whose land the street was built. South Hackney parish church, dedicated to St John of Jerusalem, provided a handsome vista for the comfortably off inhabitants. (*GJ*)

The extension of the Kingshold Estate in 1966–9 by the Greater London Council shortened King Edward Road, and the end shown here was named Moulins Road. The new Kingshold Estate was designed by architects Yorke Rosenberg Mardall, but their creation turned out to be hideous, with meandering concrete blocks connected by high level walkways. By the 1980s Kingshold had acquired a reputation as one of the worst council estates in Hackney. It has now been completely redeveloped, and the new two- or three-storey houses are much more in keeping with the rest of south Hackney, as well as looking as though they are good places in which to live. (*MK*)

Index